★A few sopranos and tenors, or solo voice.

Eight Christmas Carols (Set I)

(SEMI-CHORUS REJOIN OTHERS)

-ae! Tra - he me post te! tra - he me post te!

CHOIR (ACCOMP. TACET) Ah

Ah Ah

Ah Ah

Ah

3. O

B p legato

Ah

Pa - tris car - i - tas, O Na - ti le - ni - tas!

B mp

5

6

2. IL EST NÉ LE DIVIN ENFANT

(Born on earth the divine Christ child)

English words by
JACQUELINE FROOM

French traditional carol

Il est né le di-vin en-fant,
Born on earth the di-vine Christ child,
Jou-ez haut-bois, ré-son-nez mu-set-tes;
O-boes, re-joice, with bag-pipes vy-ing;

Il est né le di-vin en-fant,
Born on earth the di-vine Christ child,
Chan-tons tous son a-vè-ne-ment.
Sing to wel-come the Sa-viour mild.

Instrumentation: flute, 2 oboes, bassoon, 2 horns, side drum, strings.

TENORS
mp

1. De - puis plus de qua - tre mille ans Nous le pro - met - taient les pro - phè - tes,
1. 'Tis four thou - sand years and more Men his birth have been pro - phe - sy - ing;

poco rit.

De - puis plus de qua - tre mille ans Nous at - ten - dions cet heur - eux temps.
'Tis four thou - sand years and more While we longed for the joys in store.

B S. **a tempo** *p* A.

Il est né le di - vin en - fant, Jou - ez haut-bois, ré - son - nez mu - set - tes;
Born on earth the di - vine Christ child, O - boes, re - joice, with bag - pipes vy - ing;

T. *fp* *fp*

B. *fp*
(T.B. *hum*)

B **a tempo**

Il est né le di - vin en - fant, Chan - tons tous son a - vè - ne - ment.
Born on earth the di - vine Christ child, Sing to wel - come the Sa - viour mild.

2. Ah! qu'il est beau, qu'il_ est char - mant, Ah! que ses grâc - es _ sont par - fai - tes!
2. Ah! such _ beau - ty and charm a - dore! Ah! such per - fec - tion _ of grace un - dy - ing!

Ah _____ Ah _____
Ah _____ Ah _____

Ah! qu'il est beau, qu'il_ est char - mant, Qu'il est doux ce di - vin en - fant!
Ah! such _ beau - ty and charm a - dore, Pro - mised us in _ days of yore.

Ah _____ Ah _____
Ah _____ Ah _____

poco rit.

12

3. ANGEL TIDINGS

Words by JOHN RUTTER

Moravian traditional carol

Instrumentation: flute (doubling piccolo), 2 oboes, bassoon, 2 horns, glockenspiel, harp, strings.

Eight Christmas Carols (Set I)

18

4. OF THE FATHER'S LOVE BEGOTTEN

Prudentius, b. 348
tr. J. M. Neale

Melody from 'Piae Cantiones', 1582

★A few voices; may be placed distant from main body of singers.

Instrumentation: strings with organ (opt.)

A BARITONE SOLO

2. O that birth for ev - er bless - ed When the Vir - gin, full _ of

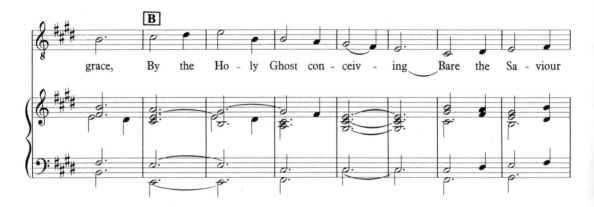

grace, By the Ho - ly Ghost con - ceiv - ing Bare the Sa - viour

of _ our race, And the Babe, the world's re - deem - - - - er,

First re - vealed his sa - cred face, *Ev - er - more and ev - er - more.*___

22